After the Reunion

Also by David Baker

Echo for an Anniversary (1992, chapbook)
Sweet Home, Saturday Night (1991)
Haunts (1985)
Summer Sleep (1984, chapbook)
Laws of the Land (1981)
Rivers in the Sea (1977, chapbook)
Looking Ahead (1975, chapbook)

After the Reunion

POEMS BY

David Baker

THE UNIVERSITY OF ARKANSAS PRESS
FAYETTEVILLE   1994

98   97   96   95   94   5   4   3   2   1

Designed by Gail Carter

The paper used in this publication meets the minimum
requirements of the American National Standard for
Permanence of Paper for Printed Library Materials
Z39.48-1984.   ⊗

Library of Congress Cataloging-in-Publication Data

Baker, David, 1954–
    After the reunion : poems / by David Baker.
        p.   cm.
    ISBN 1-55728-352-4 (cloth : alk. paper). —
    ISBN 1-55728-353-2 (paper : alk. paper)
    I. Title.
    PS3552.A4116A69   1994   94-1308
    811'.54—dc20   CIP

for Ann

Your tea is cold now.
You drink it standing up,
And leave the house.

—EDNA ST. VINCENT MILLAY

Acknowledgments

These poems, sometimes in earlier versions, appeared in the following magazines. My thanks to the editors.

The Antioch Review: "The Marriage"; *The Atlantic:* "The Couple"; *The Black Warrior Review:* "Abandoned Depot, Canada Geese," "Nemesis"; *Boulevard:* "The Deer"; *Crazyhorse:* "Piano Music," "Salvation"; *The Gettysburg Review:* "The Plain Style," "The Yard"; *The Indiana Review:* "Witness"; *The Michigan Quarterly Review:* "Car Wash at the Mall"; *The Nation:* "After the Reunion," "Trees in the Night"; *The New Criterion:* "The Accident"; *The New England Review:* "Among Men," "Missionary Position"; *The New Republic:* "Contract"; *The New Yorker:* "Faith"; *The North American Review:* "1942"; *The Ohio Review:* "Snow Figure"; *Pequod:* "Murder"; *Poetry:* "The Extinction of the Dinosaurs," "Holding Katherine," "Mercy," "Red Shift," "Taxi after an Evening Shower"; *Poetry Northwest:* "Music in the Smokehouse," "Sex," "Still Life with Jacket"; *The Seneca Review:* "Origin of a Universe"; *The Sewanee Review:* "Along the Storm Front," "Phases of the Moon"; *The Southern Review:* "Windchime"; *The Southwest Review:* "Stroke."

I also wish to thank Denison University for support during the writing of these poems.

Contents

One

Snow Figure

1.

A humble night. Hush after hush. Are you listening?
That's what the snow says, crossing the ice.

And the blue creek out back—where my love and I came
early one morning to remember nothing but blue

and the muffled joy of a far night's nothingness—
the blue creek, teasing, wild beneath its ice,

says hush. Snow whiffs around on its glassine surface.
Why did we wish so hard to walk where it deepens?

Why did we want to hold hands here?
My love and I came to learn how to love

the little that skates on the surface,
the nothing that flies, fast and fatal, beneath.

2.

I have put in a poem what has fallen from my life
and what I would change. Are you here?

We left a slender pathway of tracks. It led nowhere,
if not to our bodies, and filled in our emptiness.

What I want most to say is what I never told her.
Don't trust me. Trust me. How could I lie?

3.

A figure of speech is where desire forces a crisis, a crossing—
one world and its weather suddenly brilliant with meaning.

My love and I came out early one morning to forget
the humble one night when the snow fell over us

and we filled each other's body with our own.
So the old snow burns crystal in the sun. So the ice

slipping the creek's edges keeps teasing to be tried—
trust me, it brags, black, thrilling, or empty.

Why do we wish so hard to listen to what isn't here?
Here, the snow says, as if in response. My love was here.

The Marriage

Cupped the floating sycamore bark—cupped or curled
each sheet and flake on the slow water's shine

where the sun sifted down from high branches.
Where the sun settled down, shadow and shine, river air

wavered humid and drowsy with insects and the long
blue hush of a held breath all the way to the bend.

Our canoe knocked on the bank. We went, when we went,
skin and sore hands, willingly into the water

to soothe. Smooth the stones to our feet. A heron
settled, and rose, and settled like a wave down the distance

where the massive sycamore had fallen—flood
or the slow, insistent erosion of bank at its roots.

Not human, not tragic, its death seemed written
on each boat of bark floating, in a sentence, beyond us.

How could we stay? We rested and swam and set on
to our car waiting and work to continue.

But the heron—low its call keeps sounding through
night after night where we sleep, cupped in each other's breath.

Sweet its song. Long the nights. Far the gathering sea.

Nemesis

Below the bedpost in a dusty sphere of light
sprinkled in chaos like a slight world

torn down, the shattered tumbler had cut
his foot as he came quietly back to love.

Patches of sunlight pooled in the water
and a touch of blood on the floorboards.

Already she was laughing a little, sweeping
shards and fragments into her palm—

her back was lucent, like a sail, slender,
and she leaned to the task without blame

or visible effort to clean the mistake.
But when she looked up, he saw in her face

a small piece of doubt drawn there, as by a far,
secreted force—as by sorrow, or the gravity

that held the wild twin of their sun,
or the legend that led them to believe

each small wound would not pull them closer
to the center of privation and guilt.

Piano Music

From two stories up in the visible traces of rain,
the still steam of the city washed our window
with a blue brush. Two or three hours past midnight.
We were mood and cliché—wine on the nightstand,
stereo low, the hardwood smeared as a street.
We spun helpless in each other's grip

as we had for weeks, so quietly convinced
our love would be right, only wrong for a while,
then right. Every so often, a car or lost walker
slipped low by the window, tracks in the rain,
or one of the few streetlights popped and flickered
off and on in the sulfur and haze.

I don't recall whatever we said or didn't say.
I don't remember knowing what we had done.
It was simply late and the rain fell in the night,
and that song, so full of quiet and grief, kept finding
its way back around to our ears. Someone was gone.
That must have been why we kept playing it.

Along the Storm Front

I didn't tell you. After the killing sun
had finally started to cool back out

of the bricks, heat lightning or a far
searchlight broke the clouds scudding the low sky.

I had gone out to the wild, split hickory
to find some comfort. Its bark was peeled back,

bones sticking through. All the earlier fierce
rain rose as steam, coating the leaves a little,

hanging in the wet heat; terrible wind
had ripped the hickory.

                And then you were
beside me, swirl of your hair, your shocking

damp hand sliding along my arm, the quick,
filling desire to hold to you, the way

on the most dangerous summer days when
choking haze turns suddenly wild with wind,

dust driven up, sun and tornado can
be only minutes apart. There is no

explanation. Only the usual calm,
then the plane going down in the storm.

Abandoned Depot, Canada Geese

2:02. We had seldom been so alone—
so black was the night sky that the handful
of stars only increased its dark pressure.
The second time we heard them they must have
passed just overhead, not visible along
the rim of bare limbs nicking the skyline.
They would have been no higher than treetops—

unquestionable, the wind of two dozen wings.
It was more like a catching of breath
or a paddle working still waters, more
like linen straining on an afternoon line.
It was nothing like what it was. Why had we come?
There had not been a train in over a decade.
The first time we heard them we looked

just an instant down rusted black tracks
for the star of a headlamp leading the horn,
then back into absolute sorrow. We had seldom been
needful of each other's love. The second time.
That's when we knew what had passed, so retraced
the sound through our loss—counting as memory moves
those who pause, from two backward toward one.

Witness

What I remember is street light tipped blue on the sill.
What I remember of it could barely fill a cup.
I was kneeling—my hands and her saddening face
and the damp, sexual sheen of our bodies all a blue
spilled by the moon and the late lights out the window.

The gears of big trucks groaned low without pain.
I remember the bakery two doors down, I remember that now.
There had been rain and the rain and the cooling breads
rose as steam off the broken bricks of the street.
It entered us as breath. It left as breath

bearing a decision to leave and some need to stay longer—
a decision to leave. What I remember seems so little.
We turned inside each other's arms one more time.
Was it a star or far streetlight that blinked out just then?
I was down on my knees when the first delivery pulled away.

Stroke

In the lilac light, in the lengthening pulse of a sorrow
so profound it was nothing, a numbness, she settled
one foot for the last time in the brickway dusts.
This took no time at all. Shadow and substance
vanished in the lightening moment so near to evening.
There is a terror that starts low in the throat
and chokes out even itself. It is clear or conclusive—

the way her other foot followed as if to confirm,
like the heart's two beats complete and imprinted.
She will take this step every moment for the rest of my life.
She will not walk from the porchlight and spring again.
There is a long calm that settles every crisis.
There is a bubble in the blood, tiny and clear,
singing through the stream on its way to the brain.

Trees in the Night

With grief and finally helpless we had come to bury
the last of our love beneath the immense, swaying pines.
Months they had surrounded our sleep and our waking.
Months we had listened to their rumors of storm or of calm
so it seemed only right to grieve with them one final time—
such human grief to think they would care if they could.

There was nothing to say or so much—blame and reprisal—
it couldn't be spoken. Months we had loved
the golden finches shooting like arrows of sunlight
through branches fifty, sixty feet high. How many trees?
We stood in cool patches quiet with needles and ferns.
Such a grief—solitary, dark—still thinking of itself in the plural.

Red Shift

Only here, through the clear lens of language
and under

        the sparkling sky of a new
moon's night in a cold month, here

only
    —I have walked this far without you—

where the calm chill fractures each isolate
body like a glass,

        an emptying fear,
I have come, and stand, myself, abstract

as a star.
      All around, in the true deep

distances, the trillion trillion trillion
lovely others sail outward,

          each toward its
own blank end—shattered cells in a burst heart,

words waving
      goodbye—accelerating

in exact proportion to this moment,
darkening away

        down the visible
spectrum while I wait, here always, without you,

at the center of the extending,
                                memorial grief.

Two

Music in the Smokehouse

Fire and coal smudge. Odor of hung meat, of salt-sacks
—the slatted dark walls skinny with shelves.
Dusty light, in particles, and taped plastic windows.
Bulbless light. Odor of floor dirt and grease.

The choking soot seems, somehow, sweeter now.
And the long disorderly rows of canned fruit, the small jars
of hardware and buttons—like indices of odd jobs—
suggest care. Kept rags in trunk after trunk.

Boxes of paper. Tires. Flattened tin. I never went back.

2.

This ain't for you, boy!
But too late: I know
one uncle will bend where
another stands firm, and so sip
the tear-clear liquor
until it burns a strip straight
to my belly and set the Ball jar
back on the trunk.

Then: a bow strikes gut.
Then: lips puff into the mouth
of a sorghum jug.
Then: four thimbled fingers scrape down
on a borrowed washboard
and a beautiful song
—I can't pick out the words—
blossoms from my uncles' hard mouths.

Now *Git!* one lips, bearing down
on his banjo but grinning.
What could be sweeter
than the company of family or the sad
song's bite and balm? What grace
greater than stocking feet
buffing the floor
to a sedimentary shine?

3.

Cliché by cliché, the mind invents itself into memory.
Dearest darling, you can't know what I feel.

His yellow letter thin as dust. *Nothing like this never
happen to me before.* So I stood in the dark in the corner

and read what had floated from the rubbed-glossy pages
of the girlie magazine someone had stashed in a toolbox.

How can I tell you what I fear when I don't know myself?
What are the words? Among blonde falls and chubby tanlines

of '60s sex, the terrifying made familiar: spiders,
dust-light, and guilt. What are the words?

Nothing will keep us ever apart. I swear it.
Do you feel I am touching you now in the dark?

A rubble of secrecy and storage. *Nothing.* So I know
exactly what he meant. *It is true. I am yours.*

4.

. . . crosscut saws, and blood-rust. Odor of disuse
and the rot of wet wood. Leather. Cans of nails.
Yet it's not the boy, not him, for whom
the details align in the filtered, derivative dark,

not the pre-nostalgic boy humming through the junk.
In every corner, smoothing out the angles,
cobwebs curve with dust, thick and baggy with eggs
balanced by nothing but the thinnest of insinuations.

Only nothing says nothing. No breeze.

5.

. . . right here where I once got
my own ass whipped good . . .

(no: that's another story)

. . . here where I got kissed, once,
and so kissed back . . .

(no: another story

. . . where I hunched in the family dark
and fingered the neck of my guitar

concurrent, discordant)

until I'd memorized the song
no one wanted to hear . . .

6.

They are standing in dusk light.
They are playing and twirling.
It floats to and fro
as string-twang, as throat-puff,
as note-by-note inventions
of pleasure and fear spinning
on a staff of dust motes.
I never left. *Git ON!* and by now

he's tipsy, swinging
and jerking his big hand down
on the resonant strings.
By now: they're kicking up junk
in their glee, my aunts among shadows
shifting their underthings,
my uncles aglow. All I want is
to walk through the doorway.

7.

—Odor of the honey wagon steeping in storage.
—Potatoes in a wheelbarrow, eyeing the lazy gray light.
Of course I never went back. But that doesn't mean
they're not still hooting and mouthing a song

for themselves, crazy with everclear. It doesn't mean that.
It's what I keep hearing. A homebrew of agonies
compiled into something that seems like the past.
What else to tell you, dear darling? Please meet me.

Particles of dust. Scrap and minutiae. Bloody finger.

8.

It means I'm still waiting
for someone to let me inside.

that's another story

Come out to the smokehouse.
Don't be late. You know when.

another story

It means I'm looking for someone
whose hand will extend, exact

Git on back from there!

and with care, to touch me again
—skill of a fiddler, ear of a singer,

sawdust   pickle-brine   barrels

voice of a lost, sad lover—
and turn the rusty doorknob of the smokehouse door

wait for me, darling, reader

until it squeaks and shines,
and so turns even that opening

the first high sweet note

nothing of sound into beautiful song
for us all.

and always be yours

Three

Faith

It was midday before we noticed it was morning.
The boy cousins brought us a tray—soup and cheese,
warm soda, and a soft cloth and candy for her fever.
They wouldn't come in, the tray weighing between them.
They stood like woodwork inside the door frame.

By afternoon the old procession—silence at the lip
of a dozen night travelers tired and grieving, one
by one, or pairs floating to the bed and back
with a touching of hands like humming,
and the one we gathered for slipping farther

for all the good we could do. She lay in her shadow.
She looked to no one. Her daylilies bobbed wide
open out in the wild, blue sun and the same bee
kept nosing her window to reach them.
Dusk: even the boys were back watching it try.

1942

or 1943—but unmistakable among the tepid and long
breezes of an evening near the summer's end, that
one sense of pleasure like a fragrance
easing back the curtains, and opening out, as we rocked
from the porch wall to the white hydrangea and back—
unmistakable, the intricate, slow crinkle of paper
as she spread it to the cutting board,
the pattern fitted and pinned to the cloth.

We might sleep this evening in the swing under stars.
We might walk a while down the habitual block
and count the nighthawks cutting the dusk into pieces.
She worked her scissors down each dark line slowly;
her cotton was nearly as thin as the tissue
of her hand-me-down patterns, or the skin of her arms,
translucent, just the same brown. We could count on
the two trains to meet at the depot and wait

and never hear them depart. How soothing
the resident hum of engines at idle, at this one sense,
unmistakable in the starlight scatter and a breeze
at the brink of the trees, that no one was easing away.
When the whistle bloomed from the east, time
to sleep, she would keep stitching into night and tomorrow
one of us would have a new shirt checked blue and white
and green like the lucky, loose fitting day.

Windchime

How delicate can you make your voice still ring?
White hair, white gloves, tea in an etched clear pitcher,
the women of the family serve each other's plates,
then sit still for the story to come—the last one
fans away, diffuse from too long a telling.

Something finer always lights on the least, high branch.
Something lovely always wavers in a temporary breath.
It's as if a thumb has smeared one touch of paint
to each diamond crystal in the windchime's heart—
dash of red, mustard yellow, or a high leaf-green

centered on each cut piece. Any circumstance
will carry clear among the busy talk and silver.
How many times have you loved the same song?
Now it's the men coming down from the harvest field.
Now it's the time they marched home from war—some didn't.

Among Men

Some chore had taken me down the gravel and dust.
It would wait—first the green, mild acres mowed
to a crewcut inside the long zipper of fencing,
then everywhere like barracks the bright oil drums
popped up in perfect spacing around the farmhouse.

I saw the history of my gender standing guard
or strutting in orbit around its seclusion, one rooster
per bunker, wired by a leg with just enough play
to stretch but not breach the sphere of the next.
There were hundreds hobbled—short colonels

toeing their sand, so many bright
and brutal menfolk who would murder or mate
but never settle among others, a whole cosmos
of rogue planets held to a prudent design.
I saw my own mean spirit lean to gobble a stone—

smash the face of a friend, ruin a life.
I sped on. I did not feel but heard each shot
of gravel scratch away the surface of my car.
It was as I always knew it would be in the end—
a narrow road, a boy behind each tree.

Still Life with Jacket

1.

To find perspective in winter woods
where hill on hill is a kind of blank,
camouflage for anything, hunters
will look to snow—footprint, dimension,
ground level specified in white. What
I keep is quiet when he turns wind-
ward, tensing, glove to his open lips.

What I hold is still. All around, fog
hovers eye-high in pale fleece patches
above the drifts melting in scattered
or sudden sun. Snow keeps dusting down.
He has spotted something up-range, piled
next to the idle railroad tracks we
have followed since dawn broke. Nothing moves.

2.

In nineteen thirty-four, the poor were
everywhere migrating. They wanted,
if not a living, at least some food.
They found dust and trouble. Little work.
My retired father has led me back
where he hunted rabbits, quail, raccoon.
He has something more to say about

depression, about patience—but points.
A small arterial stream choked with
runoff is what I hear. Crush of blood.
Chill wind. It is nineteen ninety-one.

Snow shadows huddle among the bowed
silver trees as if gathered by fires—
tents, smoking pots, travelers' rubble.

3.

A little stocking cap of caked blood.
A union suit stained yellow, torn, thinned.
The man my father found had been robbed,
beaten, tossed down in the dark for dead.
His clothes, his boots were gone. His breath was
a faint flag above the cinder drifts.
That's how he spotted him, who came to,

who lived. I see the moment flit by
his eyes in a burst like sunlit wings.
There is an old jacket humped in snow
beside the tracks. It is nothing more.
How do you thank someone who slaps you
alive to the failing world? The man
kept this to himself until he died.

4.

No one forgives the living or the
dead. I don't know what to say. I lie.
The hills are thick with brown trees and white
fog aches and eases down the slivers
of streams cutting into the far slopes,
settling on the level land. I want
my father to live a longer life

than he will. I want to walk among
the rocks and waters, to find some way
to hold him. What good does wishing do?
What I keep is quiet when he walks
out in the blank and tolerant snows.
The dead are everywhere, waiting—white-
robed, huddled in the trees, trackless, cold.

The Extinction of the Dinosaurs

How much time? The old guys playing cribbage
on the back porch of the parched hotel don't have a clue.
Each truck passing on the state highway blows
Paul Harvey's voice to a murmur and a fuzz.

It's hot, it's dry, and the only growing things are
leggy goldenrods sprouting through the ribs
of one Ford chassis beside the belly-up garage.
How much time before their game is defunct, too?

One of them makes a move. Another snuffs a butt,
flicks it to the ground to circle with the rest
around a pot of dried-out mums. It's like that.
Nobody's going anywhere. Nothing's coming back.

Salvation

Someone has tapped your clenched hand and so
moves you to move—white gown and sneakers.
Someone has touched a light chord at the keyboard.
It isn't what swells the midmorning hallway
with a filtering light from the past,
and it isn't the past itself, either, come
to usher you into the sanctum of safety.

Dear god, someone says to the ceiling—dear
god comes back down in a hush. You hold still.
Someone has taken the scruff of your neck
in one hand and your hand in the other.
Now he has swept the wet hair from your eyes.
It isn't hard to be clean. It isn't the past
that has changed. It's that light, shutting off.

Taxi after an Evening Shower

This man saying *no no.* This man moaning *jesus christ.*
He's got his forehead sealed to the fogged side window
in profile to the back seat and us. He's broken.
His face, one touch from tranquil, wears the look
of weeping though it's dry—the front of the cab
glows blue, large as a cheap, cluttered room.
His friend is driving, bitten down, black stone.

But there are lights in the walls of the numinous sky.
But there are people in overcoats, dodging.
The rain has roughed up and polished the city—
blur of a blur of a blur. And so we are rushing
tight against the curb down the terminal streets,
block after block, beneath stone walls and windows
and glitter. There is only one sadness, one speed.

The Accident

He had come to tell us everything, come
so far. He stood there dazed, broken, clutching
a torn sleeve, yet calmed as by sureties
of habit or instinct. All around us
the linden trees, the dusted cedars leaned
their shag shadows into the night—the old
inhalations brushed quietly through them.
A ringlet of glass encircled his skull.
Damp blood—precise as a hatline. He had
come such a distance, really, from the last
world, it was hard to see pain on his face
until sirens began to sweep nearer.
All any of us could do was stand there,
while the locusts rocked the trees in response.

The Plain Style

Many of us carried what we could—not much.
Stars pointed out the pitiful, few clouds
as blear or ashen absences in our sky.
We strained through the ruined evening
until breath tore burning from our throats.
Sometimes disaster speaks most convincingly
in a lowered voice, his whole hand strangling

my arm, his *hurry hurry* more hiss than command.
Then the trees were in flames. Then cinders.
We could only watch the gutters run thick
with pitch and tarpaper on fire before it fell.
What had we saved? Some few clothes and pans,
pictures of elders stiff among children,
one lamp, old durable pains. Enough to summon

a plain living again though rain
would not soothe us for weeks—too late
to dampen the horror or save the spring fields.
I will never forget his huge, singed face.
Sometimes disaster sees most clearly with open
eyes raised to the sky, as in a desperate prayer
or the most serious, irreversible curse.

Mercy

Small flames afloat in a blue duskfall, beneath trees
anonymous and hooded, the solemn trees—by ones
and twos and threes we go down to the water's level edge
with our candles cupped and melted onto little pie-tins
to set our newest loss free. Everyone is here.

Everyone is wholly quiet in the river's hush and appropriate dark.
The tenuous fires slip from our palms and seem to settle
in the stilling water, but then float, ever so slowly,
in a loose string like a necklace's pearls spilled,
down the river barely as wide as a dusty road.

No one is singing, and no one leaves—we stand back
beneath the grieving trees on both banks, bowed but watching,
as our tiny boats pass like a long history of moons
reflected, or like notes in an elder's hymn, or like us,
death after death, around the far, awakening bend.

Four

Murder

Language must suffice.

Years ago,
            under a sweet June sky
stung with stars and swept back by black leaves
barely rustling,

a beautiful woman nearly killed me.

Listen,
she said,
and turned
her lovely face to the stars, the wild sky. . . .

No.

No: years ago,

            under a sweet, June sky
strung with stars and swept back by black leaves
barely rustling,

under this sky
broad, bright, all rung around

with rustling elders—or intoxicating willows,
or oaks, I forget—
            under this sky,

a beautiful woman killed me, nearly.

I say beautiful. You had to see her.

Listen,
she said,

and turned a lovely shell of her ear
to the swirl of stars
and the moon
          smudged as a wingtip in one tree, not far.

3.

Yes: she scraped my back bloody against a rough trunk.
Yes: she flung back her lovely face
and her hair, holding me down,

and the tree shook slowly, as in a mild, persistent laugh
or wind,

       and the moon high in that black tree
swung to and fro . . .

there were millions of stars
up where she stared past us,
and one moon, I think.

4.

Excuse me.

My friend, who loves poetry truly, says too much
nature taints my work.

Yes. Yes. Yes.
Too many birds, stars—
                      too much rain,
                      too much grass—
so many wild, bowing limbs
howling or groaning into the natural night . . .

and he might be right. Even here.

That is, if *tree* were a tree.
That is, if *star* or *moon* or even *beautiful woman*
craning the shell of her ear
were what they were.

They are, I think, not.

No: and a poem about nature contains anything but.

5.

When they descended to us, they were a *cloud of stars*
sweeping *lightly*. They sang to us urgently
about our lives,

they touched us
with a *hundred thousand hair-soft, small legs*—

and held down by such *hungers*, we let them cover us,
this *beautiful woman*, this *me*,

who couldn't move,
who were *stung*—do you hear?—
who were stung again, were covered that quickly, crying
to each other
          to *fly away!*

6.

      . . . I just can't erase
the exquisite, weeping language
of the wasps, nor her face in starlight
and so tranquil under that false, papery, bobbing
        moon
just minutes before,
saying listen,

listen,

nor then the weight
of her whole natural body

                              pinning down mine
until we both cried out for fear, and pain,
and *still* couldn't move.

7.

Language must suffice.
First, it doesn't. Then, of course,

it does. *Listen, listen.*

What do you hear? This nearly killed me.
I'll never know
why she didn't just whisper *Here they come,* warn *Move!*
cry *They'll kill us!*
Yes: *I will save you . . .*
Yes: *I love you too much to watch you suffer!*
But it's all I recall, or now need.

And, anyway, I loved her, she was so beautiful.
And that is what I have had to say
before it's too late,
                      before they have killed me,
before they have killed you, too,

or before we have all become something else entirely,

which is to say
before we are
only language.

Five

The Couple

Day after day their deep love softly decays.
This makes them wise. It makes them want to sing.
Sometimes, over cups in the kitchen or stirring
a fresh soup in the dark, they feel such tenderness
as to turn quietly weeping for each other's arms.
Weeping. Song. They are so much alike, after all.

The Deer

How long did we watch? How long did those
three deer stand pondering the dark, bowing to taste
the least brown grasses, the cold-burnt rose hips,
and whatever else kept alive by the creek?
I think of them each time we lie down, just so.
How still they could stand and still tremble.
They walked out of the woods in a fog.
They leaned to dry earth as to drink.
I think of them when we lie long minutes
through the reaches of winter, not lost ourselves,
not thirsty. How our bodies tense to be touched
when we forage in a scatter of blankets.

Once a man laid a deer flat with a single shot.
This gets easier to say. You open both eyes.
You let out your breath and stay still, no matter
how cold the wind, no matter how dark or how near.
The man, who is dead now, couldn't help but smile.
He walked to where the deer fell and knelt as to drink.
I think of them when we lie down in the dark.
We watched three deer lost under cedars so long
we saw the wind stand still and the ruffle of fur
behind each tense shoulder over each heart was like
our bullet digging in. That's how long. That's how still.
Until our will to love was also our power to kill.

Car Wash at the Mall

Even mud makes a halo of a steaming, still body,
and salt, cinders, snow chunked into ice, if hosed
on high pressure—all a halo sprinkling down, draining
into the circle's low center and piped to the curb.
If there is a prayer for us, perhaps it is here,
one warm day two weeks deep in December, all of us
tucked behind the mall in a line long
as an angels' train or the poor idling for food.

There is a delicate, smudged sort of rainbow
trying to stretch from one end of heaven to the corner.
If there is hope, when the human cleanses itself,
then that's why no one is fighting for a change,
angry or obviously cruel, waiting with a palmful of coins.
Spray floats around in a gauze, in a cloud . . .
and a matted dog by the curb laps the muddy pool
with a thirst so profound it brings joy.

After the Reunion

To finish by picking up pieces of cake and small clutter
from the sunporch floor, to finish by cleaning up.

We couldn't tell them—not the host of relatives
happy to be on each other's hands again,

                                         each other's nerves.
The lilac hedge let go its whole bushel of odors

and our acre's birds kept the trees stitched
with their art. Everyone agreed.

Someone's boss is somebody's neighbor.
Who looks like who in the crisp old albums?

—What kind of linen, what brand of seed, what
do you do when things get bad?

                                  There is nothing
that does not connect and so sustain.

Now I want us to keep loving each other, too.
The strength it takes is their patience—

a stretching of legs, waiting long.
Who knows what sadnesses they have endured?

Who knows which ones we have caused?
Let's open the door and let the bluejays and sparrows

attend our repair. Let's take the whole day.
Let's keep forever the napkin our last waving aunt

pressed her kiss into—delicate red, already
powdered, doomed as a rose.

Holding Katherine

Let us look up tonight where the white trees surround us.
Let us face once again the spinning stars going dim,
going cold, to stretch a while beside your one window.
Many blue arms reach down the cedars and oaks.
Like coins, brief insects glitter and toss in the glow
of streetlamps lining the lane where nobody goes for a time.

In the cradle of a new father's arms, can you hear them fall?
Once in a dream you swam in a blue dress dazzled with sun
through a garden of flowers toward me. I wrote your name
in my tablet when I woke, knowing it like the trace
of a habit handed back from the blood, knowing your face
like my own and your arms as I held you for the first time.

The star chamber swirls overhead like oceans of white hair
sparked by the wind or the tentative call of night birds
spinning their place through the tremulous dark and breeze.
Trucks groan miles distant on the highway, heading away.
You have traveled so far to be here, farther than they have
and farther than I down the winding tunnel from when time

was a speck brilliant with nothing but hope for us or despair.
Soon we will sit back to rock a while longer through
the hungry night always within us. I will sing you your name.
I will surround you with bright eyes of toys and soft sheets.
I will go quiet like this night when I go, as the light
of far stars burns in your sky from a lifetime to come.

Sex

Such joy, abundant, indiscriminate,
these easy June evenings. It's the cottonwoods

all over town and down by the bluegill
creek swollen this week by rains, like a bad

ankle: I mean, the cottonwoods all week
flinging their sex outward and down,

all the fluff and detritus of their seeds
swaying and easing onto the trim yards,

the somnolent cars, settling over
the gardens of purest cultivation

or losing themselves, fine membranes of desire,
somewhere into the winds which never seem

quite to let up. Male or female—two sure
characteristics of the cottonwood

being its unisex flower and small
catkins, or clusters of seed-bearing spikes—

it's got this news, this delirious joy.
And when all of its joy's been plentifully

broadcast, like some dreamy snow or old money,
it's got this sadness, green and down-leaning,

that only the human can love.

The Yard

Bunch grass or the months-dry wheat
and blanched-white scuff of blue and zoysia
or, in fists, in stubby tufts among the mulch,
the tubular, shiny, wild-onion grass,
wherever you look it's green sprouts, leaf-shoots.

Wherever you walk it's as if newly shod, soft
along the thaw, the edging. If this were anything
but language you could smell it,
the garlic, thick aromas of the season's first cutting
mixed among the gas- and body-fumes you shoulder

row by row, if this were what it were,
clover, bee balm, the native nouns greening
and growing, work to do. It takes all afternoon.
You'd sleep it off sore and satisfied,
onion on your hands, fresh sheets, window flung,

and the fragrance outside turns to fruit—to do again.

Origin of a Universe

The brackish smoke
of pond surface
doesn't break
no matter what

high disturbance
sets the willow
leaves to shining
or the dry, bowed

rushes to begin
to sizzle, as if
aflame, untended.
That's how long

the heat, the seem-
ing endless spell
of dryness. All
afloat in their

scum of eggs and
scorched dead leaves,
their rust-odored,
wasted, water-molded,

effluvial soup,
the suffocated
perch minnows don't
seem so misplaced,

nor the fact
that, as if some
devastating, cosmic
upheaval had

torn the whole sense
of things apart,
the pond's somehow
begun to urge

toward another
life, yet dreamed of—
and that's the strange,
nebular, gassy

sheen to it, and
that's the quiet.
Who could imagine
from such stulti-

fying nothing
might come matter,
and from matter,
in the barest

moment's massing-up,
could spring redwing
blackbirds, white-lipped
and vari-petaled

queen-anne's lace, or
the billion light-
winged mayflies which
seem to flourish

on the surface—
so much small motion
and humming, such
giddy, sweet, coming

together? Who now
cannot see, after
the slightest
thrown stone has

shattered the pure
heaven of becoming,
the wave, the news
spreading from one

precise point within
the pond's geo-
sphere, outward,
to the farthest

edge? And who
will not witness,
even now, the new
thought sinking in?

Missionary Position

For as long as we can we hold our breath.
We're watching the others, humbled

      or holding hands,
      nudge the ledge railing in pairs.

We are climbing the scenic pathway cut through old growth
pine groves and scarred granite.

      They grip whatever handrail or limb they can find.
      They cover their eyes, the better to see.

In one life it's still morning, and summer.
I lean from a deck

      over gardens in mist where you work.
      Jays ride the flat grass away.

So much weeding you don't see
yellowjackets skim the near cosmos.

      They hover an inch from your hair, rising
      wild for sweet scents from the nest at your feet.

When I touch you, your throat
closes down—veins streaking red, lungs shut.

      Days you hover in bed,
      as if winged, lingering,

your eyes turned inward to enter
a sunlit place.

> Why do we nourish what would dash us apart?
> Each time you are stung, you slip farther away.

In love, we drift down. Or go calm—
face over a face. What do you see

> when you grip my shoulders, when you come,
> softly, in sobs, shaken, unafraid?

Life after life we hold on.
The others are moving down the pathway toward home.

> In one step we see the whole world
> from above—then we are gone.

Phases of the Moon

I have walked into our midnight yard where the spruce and maples
ache to keep their shadows alive and the sweet, cut grasses
nearly glow, damp already with dew and lit as from below.
There is nothing new. The moon is only one night or two
away from its jubilant phase and I have come out
for no other reason than to need you in its blueing lights.

I have come willingly into the crisp blue world to wait.
A steady wind rinses itself in the uppermost limbs
and leaves the night lonely and cool; stars barely shine
in the trembling sky, far from the moon widening
orange and scarred through one maple's frame. I want to say
come home carefully, come home sure. Nothing is new.

Contract

People in the contracting phase [of the universe] . . .
would remember events in the future . . .
—STEPHEN HAWKING

It's the singular grace of gravity holding things up.
It's the beauty of an instant's obvious end—
the crystal lampstand leaping into light
from some fragments and dust, the rain pool waving
inward to embrace each sudden, warming drop.

Won't our lives be joyful together and often sad?
Won't the thousands more evident days and nights
burn with a future to lend us, like prophets
peering backward, a vision so true we complete it
by walking into each moment already resolved?

Stranger, my spouse, let's promise our children the world.
Let's ease into our lives with the certitude of lovers
whose futures are fact—two torn to one—and whose pasts
tighten deep into the dim, thrilling regions of art.
It's the singular gift of the present binding us now.